Sometimes a Sonnet…

poems by

Anne Johnson Mullin

Finishing Line Press
Georgetown, Kentucky

Sometimes a Sonnet…

Copyright © 2017 by Anne Johnson Mullin
ISBN 978-1-63534-112-6 First Edition
All rights reserved under International and Pan-American Copyright Conventions.
No part of this book may be reproduced in any manner whatsoever without written permission from the publisher, except in the case of brief quotations embodied in critical articles and reviews.

ACKNOWLEDGMENTS

"Afloat" and "Sonnet in Snow" appeared in *Goose River Anthology*
"Kerry Waterfall" and "Noteworthy" appeared in *Off the Coast*
"Afloat," "Kerry Waterfall," and "Noteworthy" appeared in *Surface Tension*, chapbook published by Finishing Line Press

Publisher: Leah Maines

Editor: Christen Kincaid

Cover Art: https://pixabay.com/en/red-background-abstract-macro-20137/

Author Photo: Sharon Ann Aicher

Cover Design: Elizabeth Maines

Printed in the USA on acid-free paper.
Order online: www.finishinglinepress.com
also available on amazon.com

Author inquiries and mail orders:
Finishing Line Press
P. O. Box 1626
Georgetown, Kentucky 40324
U. S. A.

Table of Contents

Sometimes a Sonnet 1
Suspension.. 2
Doves 3
Ars Poetica... 4
Reasonable... 5
Afloat.. 6
Kerry Waterfall 7
In Snow 8
Remainder 9
Noteworthy.. 10
Priapic 11
Raking Leaves 12
Thorns.. 13
Room for Humor? 14
Morality Play 15
So What?.. 16
No News Is No News 17
Haute Couture 18
Horse Sense 19
Touch.. 20
If Matthew Arnold Were Writing Now................................ 21
Time and Again 22
Back in the Day... 23
Oblivion 24
To Dust 25
Climax.. 26

Sometimes a Sonnet . . .

Some may assume the sonnet form requires
such counts of lines and feet no one desires
to write in, such restrictive rhyming schemes
in praise of love and honor as worthy themes
precluding the mundane. Thus, no oil burners
that quit, no novels touted as page turners
that aren't, no wild affairs with no beginning,
nor pitchers who can't last past the third inning.
But life turns on quotidian events;
our common nature and our common sense
deserve their share of modest celebration
while honoring tradition's strong foundation.

So—formal or relaxed in tone or measure,
sometimes a sonnet aims simply for pleasure.

Suspension

Bridges inspire wonder for the way
they fling us briefly over what we dread
falling into—rivers, slums, the gray
speed of highways, gritty railroad bed.
The longer the bridge, the greater is the tension,
the harder cables strain against collapse.
Engineers calculate precise dimensions
of slope and span to preclude any gaps

between intention and result. We cross
with confidence that aims are satisfied
by ends, that even momentary loss
of equilibrium can be denied.
Not quite the same with matters of the heart:
love leaps—but, landing, often falls apart.

Doves

The doves this morning mourn as they will do,
despite the sun-filled promise of a day
in lush mid-summer, as if to convey
their lingering sorrow for a past they rue.

Cogent psychoanalysts will say
we enter life suffering separation
from the warm nurturing ambience of gestation
and yearning for reunion all our days.

They tell us we use language as our way
to merge the self and other, but it fails
regardless of desire. Regret prevails
as words and intent never interplay
completely. Always there is something left
unsaid, unheard. Like doves we call, bereft.

Ars Poetica

It should not seem self-conscious in its rhyme
or meter, more like walking in the rain
than counting dance class steps. Yet over time
subtle refrain and measure should sustain
interest, but not beyond the fourteen lines:
too many words speak less keenly than few,
but if too few, necessity confines
ideas to a mere surface pass—like dew
upon the grass, no chance for penetration
to roots of feeling or the fledge of wings
that bear a reader beyond expectation
to realms where bold imagination sings.

And if it fails, well, hail the people who
succeed so much more admirably than you.

Reasonable

So should a sonnet rhyme at all? It should,
say some, invoking Shakespeare, Milton, Donne
and touting schemes (a-b-a-b is good).
By rules the form's deserving praise is won.
Others will say that rhythm must provide
motion to carry readers on with pleasure;
rhyme there may be, but grace must override
all sense of forced or too-difficult measure.
Content should find its form, so Coleridge pleads,
noting, with serpent's glide as metaphor,
how from each forward thrust it half recedes
then from that retrogression gains the force
to carry further forward. Undulation—
apt imagery for efforts of creation.

Afloat

The island floats this morning of calm sea
and hazy sky. We see much more of it
than in the past few days of fog. But still
only a rough-hewn shape comes into view.
On clearest days the pinpoint houses show
and shades of green and brown contour its hills.
We think we know the island then, we note
how close it seems, how keen our vision feels.
But how we fool ourselves. We cannot see
beneath the water's depth to know what holds
surface to core, hidden geology
that binds the entire planet to this spot.

And yet beneath our facile days we try
to sound a fathomless eternity.

Kerry Waterfall

And did we ever really climb that path
so spongy underfoot, and did we come
to hear the sound surround us, feel the mist
rising as rainbows underneath the falls?
Or was it all a dream and we enchanted
by the woman at the sweet shop in the town
who pointed out a most unlikely road
and told us to keep going ever higher?

Surely we did, then found the wooden sign
almost invisible in deep green brush
that led us, magic-kissed, to memorize
the glints of sun on drops of falling foam,
the roar of water pounding down the stones,
the echo calling deep within our bones.

In Snow

Walking in winter woods we pause to note
the brook that barely moves, its icy throat
muffled with frosted leaves and twigs, pinespills
soddening in passage, deadening its trills.

Whence: the word is both a question and
a way to speak of source. To understand
what hidden power maintains this tenuous flow
we must imagine warmth beneath the snow.

So even when the coldest shadows fall
and days are dark, and friends may suffer all
we think unjust, then let us think again
of source, its strength, its mystery, its small
but steady murmurs into spring, and call
upon resolve to quicken sluggish veins.

Remainder

Lava eruptions, cooled and hardened forms
dried by the sun, sculpted by wind and tide,
crusted with brine and sand solidified,
upthrust in earthquakes, scoured down by storms
and glaciers grinding slowly toward the sea,
huge coastal rock formations testify
as metaphors that poets may apply
to steady force against adversity.

And though geologists have made great gains
in fixing eras for the time it takes
for pounding seas and icy blasts to break
such massive piles, reducing them to grains
our fingers sift—our minds cannot digest
beginnings, endings, life a life-long quest.

Noteworthy

A flash of wonder questions consciousness
from somewhere near the corner of our eye—
a heron stands on one leg, motionless
among weeds in the pond as we drive by.
Or a moose moves in slow and awkward stroll
along the muddy edge of Sherman Lake,
or, there, a rumpled osprey tops a pole
above the road. We do not stop. We brake
barely enough to confirm fleeting sight
and chide ourselves for all we never see
fully, so hurried, heedless of delight
in passing, vowing from now on to be
watchful, keen, hoping not to recognize
intent as the assassin of surprise.

Priapic

Noon after snow all night and still more snow,
air a gray cloud, landscape blotter-white
absorbing all but contoured humps that show
where rocks and trees form shadows less than light.
But look—stripped of its bark, forlorn and drear,
the branchless half-trunk of a dead gray spruce
unnoticed among living trees all year
glows pink, swollen with moisture, nature's use
of phallic symbolism so out of place
it startles us. Blasting the monotone
of lifeless rounds at winter's lagging pace
it cries a truth forgotten though once known:
a life preempted should not be condemned
to absence. Passion's flare defies the end.

Raking Leaves

Last fall these leaves blew lighter than the air
that bore them out of windrows I was raking,
spreading on garden beds to insulate
perennial roots for winter hibernation.
So brittle, close to dust when trod upon,
expected to grow sodden under snow,
they should have decomposed, enriched the soil
by now and not have staged a resurrection.

But here they are this spring, so vigorous,
clogging the tines, clinging like hide to flesh
of tender shoots, displacing border rocks
I rake them from. The murderous ice, the crush
of dark and cold confinement did not kill—
instead it toughened leaves, and gardener's will.

Thorns

A thorn pulled out, the thumb hurts just until
a new sensation shifts attention. Then,
since flesh responds quite autonomically
to slight intrusions, mending goes untended.

But bruises to the psyche hardly heal.
The least-intended pressure rends the wound
scabbed tenderly after the first insult—
our birth expulsion into alien world.

Each blow that follows injures once again
the wriggling prototype of who we are:
we brood, rehash, resist, succumb anew
to pain though years go by. We pluck real thorns
no matter how ubiquitous no doubt
more gladly—knowing they will stay pulled out.

Room for Humor?

Should sonnets make us laugh? Why not? Indeed
a bit of mirth will brighten any verse
that otherwise might seem too staid or terse
to hold attention. Humor can succeed
when boredom threatens, or too serious study
to penetrate the meaning's deepest thrust
is needed, or the poem's just a bust
of no clear benefit to anybody.
Therefore a poet, I say, should have fun
and offer up, like Carroll, Lear, or Nash,
some slithy toves, some Wobblies, rhymes so brash
they surpass doggerel, they mock, they pun.
Praise nonsense that lets more sense enter in
when minds like mouths spring open with a grin.

Morality Play

We seek to do what we've been taught we ought
to do, although the way is peril-fraught
with rank temptation. Still we choose the right
and steady course, the truly noble fight.
We toil and till often against our will,
we scarce indulge, let alone take our fill
of candy, booze, or sex lest we be thought
rank hedonists, which, thank the Lord, we're not,
nor too self-righteous, either, God forbid!
We're only reining in our wayward id
in case we face harsh judgment when we die.
If not, we'll rue missed chances to defy
the odds that say we're doomed to come to naught
for seeking what we're taught that we ought not.

So What?

So on the evening news, interviewees:
"So, Gwen, the talks broke down. . . ." "So, if the Saudis . . ."
"So, pollsters say . . . " "So, no one really knows . . ."
The "so" presumes some continuity
if not cause and effect, where none exists.
We hear the "so" as throat-clearing reflex
the way "um," "like" and "you know" used to serve
the Valley Girls and all their breathless ilk
"for sure." So now we have the So and Sos
pretending to refer their statements to
some sense that lies beyond what seems like so
much nonsense that a listener will stop
trying to hear. There may be truth somewhere
but all these "so"s are robbing it of air.

No News Is No News

It's not news when the anchor persons tease
viewers with a promise to reveal
some shocking international oil deal
or feel-good tale of migrant kids and cheese
"after the break," so we'll stay tuned through ads
for Kias, carpeting, molar implants,
furniture blow-out sales and tall men's pants
spaced around fluff segments on new fads
like pontoon bike-racing, before we hear
again the broadcast team will "be right back."
Finally two sentences with seconds tight:
"OPEC says NO oil deal is near"
and "Studies show that migrant diets lack
protein, like that in cheese." That's it? Good night!

Haute Couture

Our fashionista days may well be over
and spike-heeled sandals way beyond our dreams.
Gone are the times we might have rolled in clover
with hot pants on or off, wild though it seems.
But still we check out styles, with dread and wonder
at "new" trends we recall from prior seasons
as being *très* unfit for now. We ponder
all those we have abandoned with good reason:
short skirts that show off all-too-fleshy thighs,
sleeveless cuts revealing arm-flab swinging,
waist-roll-baring low-slung jeans, and size-
too-small silk knits, so sleekly body-clinging.
We've learned (and hope young gals won't take offense)
to damn that oxymoron, *fashion sense!*

Horse Sense

"Horses can't spell, anyway," said the lady
who transposed "a-o" in American Pharoah
and won the contest to christen the horse
that went on to claim racedom's prized Triple Crown.

But how does she know that horses can't spell?
They can count, as we've seen on TV when they hoof
the number of apples or balls in a bucket,
so why not assume they can recognize letters?

And thus learn to spell from constant exposure
to their names on blankets and over their stalls,
on racing forms, too, when their trainers peruse them?
So American Pharoah, upset not at all
by the gaffe on the victory cup on his shelf.
can horse-laugh—he's made quite a name for himself!

Touch

The ladies told of how they'd been to Raiki,
a demonstration at a nearby spa.
One talked excitedly about the moment
she felt her mother's hand in hers and heard
that long-stilled voice, so powerful the presence
she struggled to regain her present tense.
I know whose hand I'd feel in meditation,
even without deep thought, my Grandma Beth's,
her steel-trap grip around my wrist whenever
she took me to "do errands" at the grocer's,
the Five & Ten, phone company, the bank,
the creamery for butter and milk sherbet,
a cone for me, a quart to carry home.
She'd let go then. I still retain her touch.

If Matthew Arnold Were Writing Now

Listen, said Arnold, to the grate and roar
of pebbles raked by waves at Dover Beach;
for him the ebbing tide a metaphor
for waning faith in God's protective reach.
But if he lived today Arnold's lament
might focus on hard data from the sea
itself, its temperatures and sediments,
its creatures, habitats no longer free
from taint. He'd worry not lest science alter
human morality of thought and deed,
but that it won't! He'd watch the breakers falter
roiled by a noxious undertow of greed.
He'd rouse our faith in science to counteract
the toxic flux, no metaphor but fact.

Time and Again

We should not put such weight upon the hours
that flow from sunlight and the moon's events
of days and months—such arbitrary powers
conferred on calendars lack pertinence.
A day, a week, a year will hardly show
the truth of what life means, and yet we look
to schedule living minutes when we know
that love and death keep no appointment book.

Some people say, as if it were a fact,
that time is money, that it runs so fast
to waste it is a crime. It won't come back.
But when we relive pleasures long since past
we validate with retrospect sublime
the liberating timelessness of time.

Back in the Day

The Red Sox had a pitcher named Mc Dermott.
Maury, a southpaw, six foot three and skinny,
barely eighteen when he signed with Boston.
A bit wild, threw more balls than strikes, too often
he'd run the count to three and two, then walk
the batter, force a bases-loaded run
or brace for a grand slam. Sometimes he'd strike
somebody out, or double-plays might end
the inning. I would listen with my father
in agony through every pitch because
I had a crush on him. I'd met him once
and so I rooted faithfully though sadly.
I had to learn that rooting's not enough
unless a would-be hero's got the stuff!

Oblivion

Where do they go when they are gone, the small
flitters of mind that flicker in the brain
for moments, the ephemera of rain
so light it vanishes even as it falls.
An EEG can carry out a scan
illuminating dendrites' pulse and glow,
charged ions in their systematic flow,
but sensors fail to show the final plan
by which an impulse travels to become
a full-fledged inspiration, an idea
beyond an image, something far more clear
to grasp, to think about, a depth to plumb
in search of even one aborted thought
that might have mattered— had we not forgot.

To Dust . . .

A sense of duty moves the feather duster
made not of feathers but some ersatz down
that flicks the dust efficiently enough
so slats of blinds, the knick-knack shelves and tops
of end-tables look better as she passes
from one room through another thinking how
dust does not reveal itself when coating
each surface evenly all undisturbed
but take one item from its place and then
where it just was becomes a graphic loss.

So she is careful not to disarrange
the folded reading glasses or the line
of graduated conch shells she could never
form in that curve exactly as he left them.

Climax

Hard to detect the point at which the tide
reverses neap to ebb; nothing betrays
the act occurring, only afterviews
of covered or uncovered rocks reveal
the changed direction.
                      Nor can one predict
precisely when a mounting wave will crest:
the foam that forms just as the edge begins
to curl obscures the moment of its fall.

How, then, to find the turning points of time
we live within? While months and years flow on
we think to weigh their consequence, we try
to gauge the peaks and troughs but finally know
the high point of a life cannot be treasured
until the end allows it to be measured.

Anne Johnson Mullin is currently re-retired to Bonita Springs, FL, from New Harbor, Maine. She fell in love with sonnets as a Tufts University English major (class of 1958) in Prof. Harold Blanchard's classes, but wrote them only occasionally over the years, preferring free verse, forgetting how much fun it can be to play with the 14-line form and its conventions.

Anne taught composition at the Universities of Maine and Massachusetts while earning her M.A. and Ph.D. respectively, and then at Idaho State University in Pocatello, where she also directed the Writing Center. Anne had previously served as Alumni Director at the University of Maine at Farmington for many years. Her career has included stints as a humor columnist for the *Franklin Journal* (Farmington, ME), *Harvard University Football News*, and the Westwood (MA) *Transcript Press*.

Her poems have appeared in the *Atlanta Review, Comstock Review, Puckerbrush Review, Sow's Ear Review, Off the Coast, Goose River Anthology* and *Common Ground Review*, among other publications. Finishing Line Press published her chapbook, *Surface Tension*, a Starting Gate Award winner, in 2006.

www.ingramcontent.com/pod-product-compliance
Lightning Source LLC
LaVergne TN
LVHW041520070426
835507LV00012B/1704